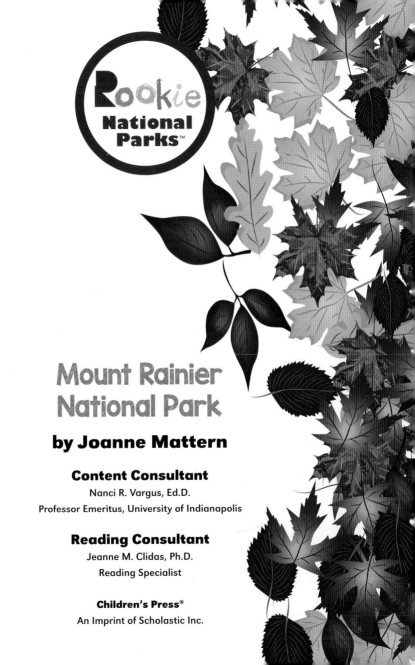

Rookie
National
Parks™

Mount Rainier National Park

by Joanne Mattern

Content Consultant

Nanci R. Vargus, Ed.D.
Professor Emeritus, University of Indianapolis

Reading Consultant

Jeanne M. Clidas, Ph.D.
Reading Specialist

Children's Press®
An Imprint of Scholastic Inc.

Library of Congress Cataloging-in-Publication Data

Names: Mattern, Joanne, 1963– author.
Title: Mount Rainier National Park/by Joanne Mattern.
Description: New York, NY: Children's Press, an imprint of Scholastic Inc., 2018. | Series: Rookie national parks | Includes bibliographical references and index.
Identifiers: LCCN 2017060551| ISBN 9780531126530 (library binding) | ISBN 9780531189047 (pbk.)
Subjects: LCSH: Mount Rainier National Park (Wash.)—Juvenile literature.
Classification: LCC F897.R2 M39 2018 | DDC 979.7/782—dc23
LC record available at https://lccn.loc.gov/2017060551

Produced by Spooky Cheetah Press
Design: Ed LoPresti Graphic Design
Creative Direction: Judith E. Christ for Scholastic Inc.

Published in 2019 by Children's Press, an imprint of Scholastic Inc.

Printed in Heshan, China 62

Scholastic, Inc., 557 Broadway, New York, NY 10012.

Photos ©: cover: Art Wolfe Stock/Robert Harding Picture Library; back cover: Ji-fang Zhang/Getty Images; "Ranger Red Fox" by Bill Mayer for Scholastic; 1-2: PCRex/Shutterstock; 3: D.C. Lowe/Getty Images; 4-5: Spaces Images/Getty Images; 6-7: NaturaLight - No Release Needed/Alamy Images; 7 inset: Heath Korvola/Getty Images; 8 inset: NASA; 8-9: Jeremy Woodhouse/Getty Images; 10-11: Tom Sayles/Flickr; 11 inset: John Mayer/Flickr; 12-13: july7th/iStockphoto; 14-15: Kelly vanDellen/Shutterstock; 16 inset: Leonard Rue Enterprises/Animals Animals; 16: Walter Arce/Dreamstime; 17: Gerrit Vyn/age fotostock; 18 top: step2626/iStockphoto; 18 bottom: Calvin Larsen/Science Source; 19: Konrad Wothe/Minden Pictures; 20 inset: Thomas & Pat Leeson/Science Source; 20-21: Gerrit Vyn/Minden Pictures; 21 inset: randimal/Getty Images; 22 inset: Ron_Thomas/iStockphoto; 22-23: chinaface/iStockphoto; 24-25: Marc Pagani/Aurora Photos; 25 inset: Aaron Mccoy/Robert Harding Picture Library; 26 top left: Mikael Males/Dreamstime; 26 top center: Chris Mattison/Minden Pictures; 26 top right: Isselee/Dreamstime; 26 bottom left: GlobalP/iStockphoto; 26 bottom center: JackF/iStockphoto; 26 bottom right: Nick Saunders/Minden Pictures; 27 top left: MediaFuzeBox/Shutterstock; 27 top center: dmodlin01/iStockphoto; 27 top right: Willard/iStockphoto; 27 bottom left: Bob_Eastman/iStockphoto; 27 bottom center: Dave King/Getty Images; 27 bottom right: GlobalP/iStockphoto; 30 top left: Dorling Kindersley/Getty Images; 30 top right: zoomstudio/iStockphoto; 30 bottom left: Melinda Fawver/Dreamstime; 30 bottom right: Matthew Ward/Getty Images; 31 top: rickszczechowski/Getty Images; 31 center top: Bjulien03/Dreamstime; 31 center bottom: Beboy_ltd/iStockphoto; 31 bottom: Royal Freedman/Alamy Images; 32: Keenan Harvey/Aurora Photos.

Maps by Jim McMahon/Mapman ®.

Table of Contents

I am Ranger Red Fox, your tour guide. Are you ready for an amazing adventure in Mount Rainier?

Welcome to Mount Rainier National Park!

Mount Rainier (**ruh**-neer) is in Washington State. It is named for the giant mountain that towers over the park. Mount Rainier became a **national park** in 1899. People visit national parks to enjoy nature.

United States

←Washington

Mount Rainier
National Park

N
W ◆ E
S

There are so many cool things to see in this park! Rainier is the highest mountain in the state. And it is surrounded by fields of flowers, thick forests, rivers, lakes, and waterfalls. There are even **glaciers** and ice caves here. Many types of animals live in this special place.

Mount Rainier is part of the Cascade mountain range.

It takes two days to climb Mount Rainier. Only experienced climbers can make the trek.

This photo of Mount Rainier was taken from space!

Scientists keep an eye on Mount Rainier. If the volcano were to show signs of erupting, they would warn people!

Chapter 1

Fiery Mountain

You might not know it by looking, but there is something special about this mountain. It is a volcano! It has openings through which **lava**, hot gases, and ash can explode. The last time Mount Rainier erupted was in 1894. Today, it is **dormant**.

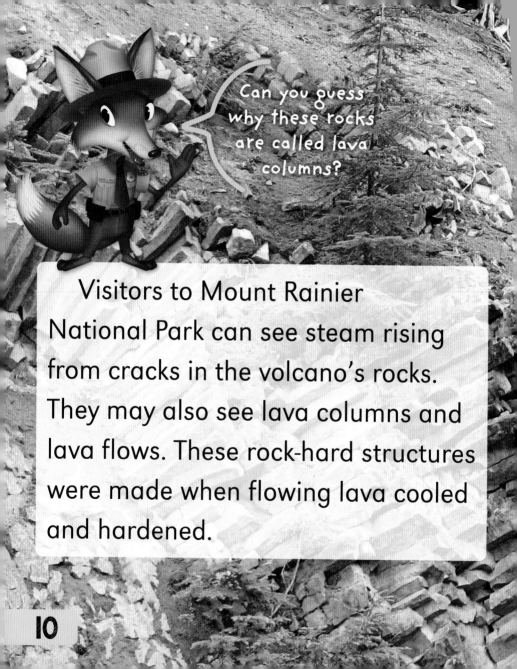

Can you guess why these rocks are called lava columns?

Visitors to Mount Rainier National Park can see steam rising from cracks in the volcano's rocks. They may also see lava columns and lava flows. These rock-hard structures were made when flowing lava cooled and hardened.

Do you see the steam escaping from the rocks? The inside of a volcano is superhot!

Emmons has the largest surface area of any glacier in the United States outside of Alaska.

Chapter 2

The Big Chill

There are 25 glaciers in the park. The Emmons Glacier is the biggest. Long ago, it stretched 40 miles (60 kilometers) long. Today, the Emmons Glacier covers more than 4 square miles (10 square kilometers). That's about the size of 2,000 football fields.

Mount Rainier also has many ice caves. They form when hot steam from the volcano melts some of the thick ice. Visitors to the caves can walk beneath thick layers of sparkling glacial ice.

The park has the largest volcanic glacier cave network in the world.

Mountain goats easily climb high on the mountainside.

Bobcats hunt birds and other small animals in the forests.

16

Chapter 3

Amazing Animals

Mount Rainier National Park is home to animals of all shapes and sizes. Mountain lions and black bears can be found here, as can bobcats and red foxes. Visitors may also see deer, mountain goats, porcupines, and even little jumping mice!

Black bears roam throughout the park.

Many kinds of birds live in the park, too. At night, spotted owls and barred owls hoot from the tall trees. Songbirds like the

northern spotted owl

willow flycatcher feast on seeds and insects in the grasses of the meadows. Waterfowl glide through the park's lakes and ponds.

This is a family of trumpeter swans.

Steller's jays often hang around picnic areas looking for food!

The northern spotted owl is the only endangered bird that permanently lives in the park.

Frogs, toads, snakes, and lizards hop, slither, and crawl in Mount Rainier. There are salamanders, too.

The Cascades frog is named for the mountains where it lives.

The Pacific giant salamander can grow to be 12 inches (30 centimeters) long! It is big enough to eat mice and snakes.

Salmon swim in many of the park's streams.

Chapter 4

Green and Growing

Thick forests are found at the base of Mount Rainier. Firs, pines, and cedars grow there. Farther up the mountain, you can find meadows filled with wildflowers. The flowers make a carpet of bright colors.

Rainier's wildflowers usually bloom in middle to late summer.

This hiking trail is next to Tipsoo Lake.

A meadow is a large grassy field.

There are plenty of things for kids to do in Mount Rainier National Park. You can hike or bike along 50 trails to see the beautiful meadows and forests. You can boat, fish, and even camp above the clouds. You can explore ice caves and waterfalls. Someday, maybe you can even climb to the top of Mount Rainier!

Skiers can usually find snow in Rainier from November through June!

Imagine you could visit Mount Rainier. What would you do there?

These are just some of the incredible animals that make their home in Mount Rainier.

fisher

green tree frog

porcupine

mountain lion

mountain goat

willow flycatcher

Wildlife by the Numbers

The park is home to about...

182 types of birds

65 types of mammals

If you're lucky, you might see a red fox like me in the park!

elk

coyote

Chinook salmon

bobcat

black bear

Cascade red fox

19 types of reptiles and amphibians

14 native fish species

Where Is Ranger Red Fox?

Oh no! Ranger Red Fox has lost his way in the park. But you can help. Use the map and the clues below to find him.

1. Ranger Red Fox started at the top of Mount Rainier.

2. Then he slid down Emmons Glacier.

3. Next, he walked southeast to go hiking in the forest on the Summerland Trail.

4. Finally, he walked southwest to meet some friends for a picnic.

Help! Can you find me?

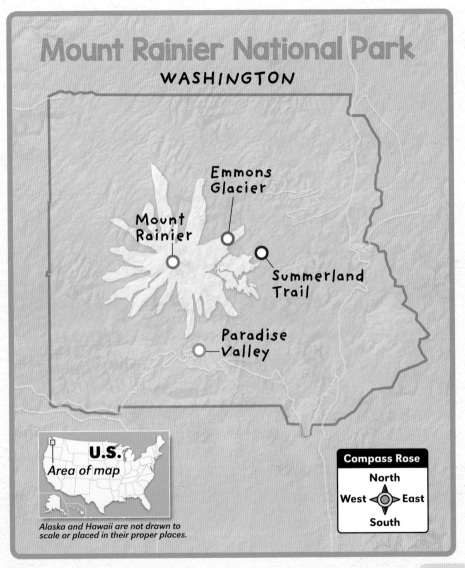

Mount Rainier National Park
WASHINGTON

Emmons
Glacier

Mount
Rainier

Summerland
Trail

Paradise
Valley

U.S.
Area of map

*Alaska and Hawaii are not drawn to
scale or placed in their proper places.*

Compass Rose

North

West ◄◆► East

South

Can you guess which leaf belongs to which tree in Mount Rainier? Read the clues to help you.

A.

1. Cedar
Clue: The needles on this tree look like soft feathers.

B.

2. Hemlock
Clue: This tree has brown cones that hang from its branches.

C.

3. Red alder
Clue: The leaves of this tree are wide and green.

4. Fir
Clue: This tree has lots of green needles instead of leaves.

D.

30

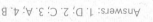

Glossary

dormant (**dor**-muhnt):
not showing any signs of
activity but capable of
becoming active again

glaciers (**glay**-shurz):
huge blocks of slow-moving ice

lava (**lah**-vuh):
hot, liquid rock that pours out
of a volcano when it erupts

national park (**nash**-uh-nuhl
pahrk): area where the land
and its animals are protected
by the U.S. government

Index

Facts for Now

Visit this Scholastic Web site for more information
on Mount Rainier National Park:
www.factsfornow.scholastic.com
Enter the keywords **Mount Rainier**

About the Author

Joanne Mattern has written more than 250 books for children.
She likes writing about natural wonders because she loves to
learn about the amazing places on our planet and the animals
and plants that live there. Joanne grew up in New York State and
still lives there with her husband, four children, and several pets.